Cotswold Villages

Photographs by Stephen Dorey

Text by John Mannion

MYRIAD

LONDON

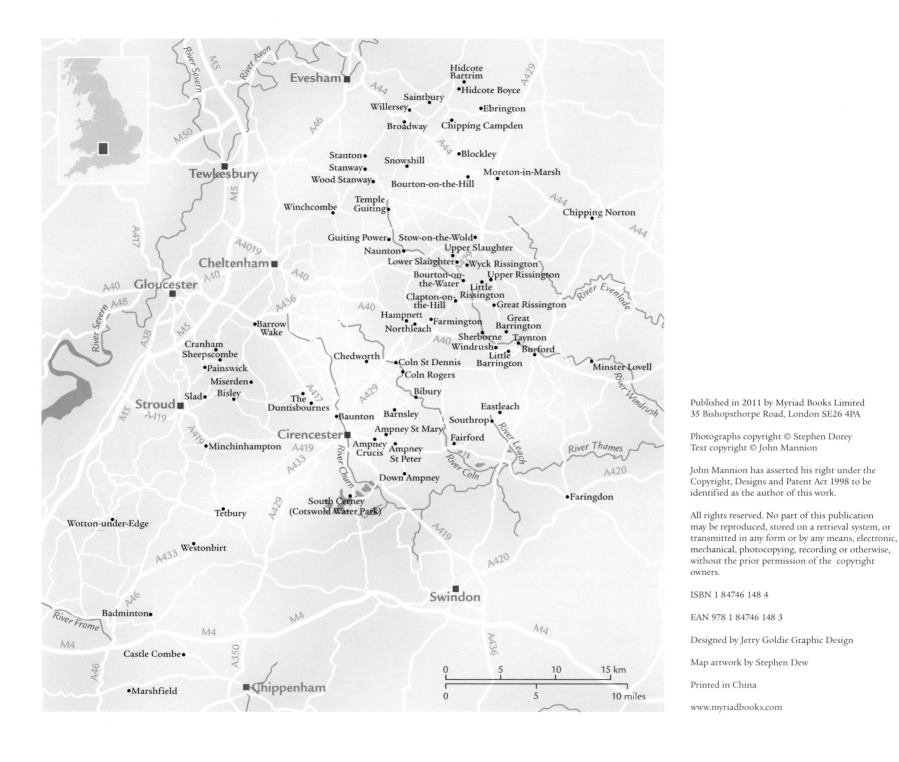

Published in 2011 by Myriad Books Limited
35 Bishopsthorpe Road, London SE26 4PA

Photographs copyright © Stephen Dorey
Text copyright © John Mannion

John Mannion has asserted his right under the
Copyright, Designs and Patent Act 1998 to be
identified as the author of this work.

ISBN 1 84746 148 4

EAN 978 1 84746 148 3

Designed by Jerry Goldie Graphic Design

Map artwork by Stephen Dew

Printed in China

www.myriadbooks.com

CONTENTS

THE AMPNEYS

The three villages of Ampney Crucis, Ampney St Mary and Ampney St Peter, just east of Cirencester, take their name from the small river, a tributary of the Thames, on which they stand.

The diverse styles of the Holy Rood church in Ampney Crucis (below right) reflect its chequered past but the grounds preserve a rare 15th century cross that was hidden from the Puritans by being walled up inside the building. The church at Ampney St Mary (below) is isolated from its village possibly because the original settlement declined as a result of the Black Death. The small hamlet of Ashbrook now carries the name of the church. Ampney St Peter (below middle) is the third village in this group. Its church is mostly Saxon in design with some Victorian additions; the grounds contain a carved pre-Christian fertility symbol. The largest house in the area is Ampney Park. This was constructed by the Pleydell family in 1561 and significant additions were made in the 18th and 19th centuries. It has an extremely well preserved Jacobean ceiling. The close proximity of the three villages and their sites make the Ampneys a popular destination for walkers and ramblers.

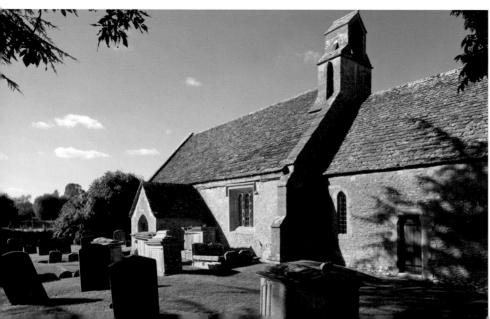

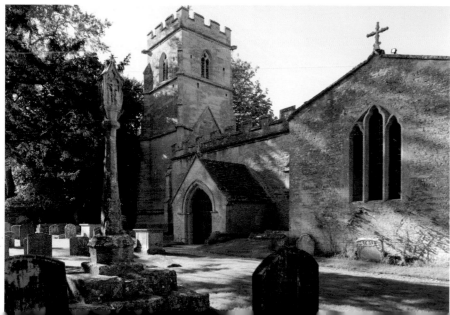

BADMINTON

Situated just east of Chipping Sodbury, the pretty village of Badminton lies close to Badminton House, seat of the Dukes of Beaufort.

Badminton is an estate village which grew up serving the needs of nearby Badminton House. The bulk of the houses in the present village date from the late 18th and early 19th centuries and there are several thatched cottages. Within the village Essex House, the Old Vicarage, the Cottage and the High Street Pump Cottages are Grade II listed as are many of the distinctive farm buildings beyond it. The local vernacular architecture, in Cotswold stone, works well with the open land-scape of the area. Badminton House is the home of the Beaufort family and is a particularly fine

example of the Palladian period. The park is partly the work of Lancelot "Capability" Brown and contains a Great Avenue that is several miles long. It is 15,000 acres in size with herds of fallow and red deer. The game of badminton was invented here. Badminton House is famous for its International Horse Trials.

BARNSLEY

Barnsley village, north-east of Cirencester, is chiefly noted for Barnsley House Garden. This project, begun in the 1950s, has attracted interest from all over the world.

Barnsley House itself dates from 1697 when it was built for a local landowner, Brereton Bouchier. It spent much of its history thereafter as a parsonage but its fame began to develop in the 20th century when its gardens came under the care of Rosemary Verey. Working by instinct rather than formal plan she recreated a variety of different garden types including an 18th century herb

garden, a knot garden, a laburnum walk, a temple with a pool and a vegetable garden. The gardens, which inspired the Prince of Wales in his own efforts in this area at nearby Highgrove House, are accessible through group tours and for occasional open days. Barnsley House is now an exclusive hotel and spa. Beyond the village is Barnsley Park which houses a fine Georgian mansion.

BAUNTON

Baunton, three miles north of Cirencester, has been described as "an unadorned Cotswold hamlet, beautiful in its simplicity".

Situated on the river Churn, the village is referred to in the Domesday Book and parts of its church are of Norman origin. The Manor House dates from the 16th century and the original village school, which operated from 1849 until 1935, can

still be seen at the Old School House. Other listed buildings in the village include Baunton Mill and Downs Farmhouse. The church of St Mary Magdalene, built originally as a chapel of ease by Augustinian monks, became the parish church in 1551 following the Dissolution of the Monasteries. Its shape and character have changed little over the years and the building preserves a large 14th century wall painting of St Christopher ferrying the Christ Child across a river. In addition there is a rare pre-Reformation Early English altar frontal. A number of ancient routes cross the parish of Baunton including the Whiteway and

the Welsh Way while to the east and west respectively are the Roman roads the Fosse Way and Ermin Way.

BIBURY

In the 1870s William Morris pronounced Bibury, to the north-east of Baunton, the most beautiful village in England. It has lost none of its charm in the intervening years.

The settlement dates back to Saxon times and its church still retains some Saxon features; the bulk of the present village owes its existence to the 17th century wool trade. Arlington Row is a terrace of weavers' cottages that was built to house workers from Arlington Mill at the other end of the village. Rack Isle, in front of the cottages and now a bird sanctuary, was formerly used for drying wool. Arlington Mill is now a museum of rural life. The Coln river which runs through Bibury is famous for its trout but visitors are more likely to catch fish at the Bibury Trout Farm. St Mary's church was restored by the architect Gilbert Scott in 1863 and it is possible to see "before" and "after" pictures in the Arlington Mill Museum. The "restoration" attempted to make the exterior look more medieval but most of the modifications took place in the interior where

such things as box pews were replaced by more simple kneelers. A new stone and marble pulpit was added as was a fine brass lectern. In Bibury churchyard can be found the Bisley Piece. Apparently the people of Bisley angered a 14th century pope who forbade them to bury their dead in their own churchyard, so for two years local people had to travel 15 miles to use the Bibury churchyard.

BISLEY

The many fine houses in and around Bisley, five miles north-east of Stroud, are a testament to the wealth of the cloth trade.

Amongst the finest of the clothiers' houses are Over Court, with its gazebo overlooking the churchyard, and Jaynes Court but there are many more modest but no less fine buildings scattered throughout the village. The church of All Saints has an imposing spire and a unique hexagonal "Poor Soul's Light" in the churchyard. This 13th century structure was used to hold mass candles for those who could not afford candles of their own; it is the only outdoor example in the country. At one end of the village are five water chutes known locally as "the Wells"; they were restored as wells to commemorate the reverend Thomas Keble, brother of John, who was rector of Bisley for nearly 50 years. As was common in many Cotswold communities the village has a small 19th century two person lock-up; with its S-shaped gables Bisley's is a fine example.

BLOCKLEY

Blockley, four miles north-west of Moreton-in-Marsh, was one of the first villages in England to produce its own electricity thanks to the power of the Blockley Brook.

This village and the surrounding pasture land was owned by the bishops of Worcester. The brook provided the energy for cornmills, silk throwers and even wood saws. At the height of the silk boom in the late 19th century there were six mills in operation and around 600 people were employed in the trade. One mill can still be seen beyond a pool near the church and the beautiful Mill Dene garden has been created around another one. Many of the terraced cottages on the village's northern edge were once occupied by silk weavers. Parts of the church date from the Norman period but the tower was only added in 1725 by local quarry owner Thomas Woodward. In the church is a series of handsome monuments to local landowners and some interesting brass monuments dedicated to former parish priests.

BOURTON-ON-THE-HILL

Two miles west of Moreton-in-Marsh, Bourton-on-the-Hill was once owned by the abbots of Westminster who also had large sheep runs on the nearby Bourton Downs.

The wealth created by the 15th century wool industry enabled the building of a particularly fine clerestory window in the church. The three-stage tower also dates from the Perpendicular period but the weighty arched columns of the interior reveal its Norman origins. The church also preserves a bell-metal bushel and peck from 1816. These standard measures were once required by law in every church so that they could be used for the gathering of tithes and for settling disputes. At the top of the hill is a substantial 18th century coaching inn. The village also contains many fine 17th and 18th century cottages.

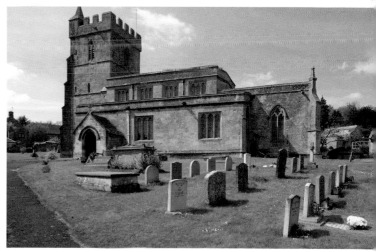

BOURTON-ON-THE-WATER

Five ornamental bridges span the river Windrush in Bourton-on-the-Water,
four miles from Stow-on-the-Wold.

Moving downstream, the five bridges are: Bourton Bridge built in 1806 and widened in 1959; Mill Bridge (also known as Broad Bridge) built in 1654 on the site of a former ford; High Bridge, a footbridge built in 1756; New Bridge (or Moore Bridge) built in 1911 to traverse another ford and Coronation Bridge, built in 1953 to replace a wooden bridge. Other attractions in this popular village include the Dragonfly Maze, with over a quarter of a mile of pathways and an attractive pavilion at its centre; Birdland, a bird sanctuary that includes a small colony of penguins; the Cotswolds Motor Museum; and the Model Village which is a small-scale replica in Cotswold stone of Bourton complete with its own model village. Bourton-on-the-Water also has a model railway exhibition and Miniature World, a collection of tiny scenes created by Britain's best model-makers. On a larger scale, visitors can see exhibitions of pottery in Little Clapton Row and an exhibition of village life housed in a former mill. On the edge of the village is a series of flooded gravel pits which have been established as a nature reserve and contain varied collections of birdlife.

BROADWAY

This showpiece village, six miles south-east of Evesham, has a wide main street. The village was once an important staging post on the London to Worcester route.

A new turnpike road was opened in 1736 and at one time seven coaches passed through the village each day. Many of the fine buildings along Broadway's main street began their lives as inns to serve the passing trade. With the coming of the railways the coach trade died away but Broadway had its own station and it quickly became a stopping off point for exploration of the Cotswolds. The village was a particular favourite of William Morris (who stayed at Broadway Tower) and other members of the Arts & Crafts movement who often preferred bicycles as a means of transport.

Above: the splendid folly of Broadway Tower was built at the end of the 18th century by James Wyatt at a spot on Broadway Hill used for centuries as the site of a signal beacon

BURFORD

Burford built its reputation on wool, quarrying and coaching but nowadays it is regarded as the eastern gateway to the Cotswolds.

Wool was important from the 14th century onwards and the stone from quarries near Burford was used to construct some of Britain's finest buildings, ranging from Blenheim Palace to St Paul's cathedral. Burford's heyday as a coaching town came in

the 18th century when it was an important stop on routes to Oxford and London; "Burford Bait", the huge meals served by the inns, were famous in the region. Sadly, the coaching trade died away with the advent of the railways which also bypassed the town. Burford's steep High Street with its many inns is well known but there are many other delightful buildings and features away from the main street. These include the 15th century church, the 17th century Great House and a row of handsome almshouses. The church is interesting both architecturally and historically. One memorial carving

includes the first representation of Amazonian Indians in England and the font preserves the autograph of a Leveller prisoner held in the church during the Civil War.

Castle Combe

Five miles north-west of Chippenham, Castle Combe lies to the south of the area generally regarded as the Cotswolds. But this pretty village displays many of the charms of the area and is a popular destination for visitors.

The village is centred on a market cross that reflects its growth through wool-trading. Other marks of this once great industry

include several fine timber-framed buildings clustered around the cross and the substantial Perpendicular tower that was added to the church in 1434. The village is situated on the By Brook and there is a charming bridge that spans the

stream here. In 1966 this section of the brook was converted into a miniature port complete with jetty and boats for the filming of *Dr Doolittle* starring Rex Harrison. The Norman castle that gives the village its name has largely disappeared but the mound on which it was built is still present. There are many fine walks in the area and the village is on the Macmillan Way long-distance footpath. Also near the village is the Castle Combe motor-racing circuit.

CHEDWORTH

Eleven miles south-east of Cheltenham, Chedworth, in the Coln valley, combines the ancient and modern.

Opposite the venerable Seven Tuns inn a spring emerges from a wall whilst elsewhere in the village there is a modern sculpture of the Virgin and Child carved by Helen Rock in 1911. The church retains some Norman features but it has been sensitively added to over the centuries. Not far from the village is Chedworth Roman villa. Discovered

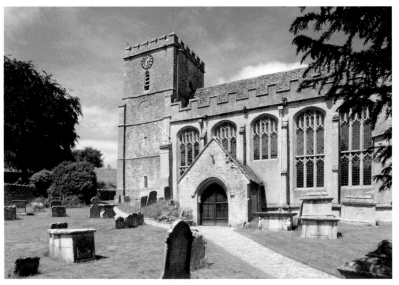

in 1864 it is one of the finest Roman villas in Britain. Dating from 120-400 AD, the beautifully preserved remains include mosaic pavements, bath suites and a hypocaust. There is a small museum nearby where visitors can learn more about the history of the site.

CHIPPING CAMPDEN

The word "chipping" relates to an Old English word meaning market and it was as a wool and cattle market that this fine village, 10 miles south-east of Evesham, first developed.

Grevel House (bottom right, overleaf) was built for William Grevel in about 1380 and features striking Perpendicular style two-storey windows. It is one of many fine houses from this period that adorn the village. The Market Hall was built in 1627 by Sir Baptist Hicks; it was intended for the sale of cheese, butter and poultry in a period when the wool trade was in decline.

In 1612 Hicks had commissioned the row of almshouses just below St James' church; they originally cost £1,000 and are still used today to house 12 Campden pensioners. Next to the church are the lodges and gateway to Sir Baptist Hicks' residence, Campden House (photograph overleaf). These are survivors of a number of original buildings – the rest were burned down during

the Civil War. St James' church is a significant local landmark. It is built in the Perpendicular style and features a 15th century pinnacled tower. Its interior houses some interesting marble monuments, several monumental brasses and an excellent collection of English medieval embroidery. In the early 20th century Charles Ashbee moved his Guild and School of Handicraft to Chipping Campden from London. The Guild specialised in metalworking, producing jewellery, enamels, hand-wrought copper, wrought ironwork and furniture. This brave social experiment did not survive the Depression but it began the process of regeneration of today's village.

CLAPTON-ON-THE-HILL

This small village is situated on a hill overlooking the valley of the river Windrush, three miles south of Bourton-on-the-Water.

✍

Not far from the centre of the village, beyond its tiny three-sided village green, is Clapton Manor. This substantial three-storey 16th century building has thick walls and solid oak beams; it is surrounded on three sides by well-tended and varied gardens. The interior retains many period features such as mullioned windows and inglenook fireplaces. It is now open as a small hotel. The parish church of St James' dates from the late 12th century and is one of the smallest in the Cotswolds. It still preserves some 12th and 13th century features including a tiny lancet window above the altar, a south doorway with a plain tympanum and a tub font. Many of the windows are from the Tudor period having survived the Civil War.

The churchyard gates are made from old horseshoes. Its many fine views make Clapton-on-the-Hill popular with ramblers and it is on the North Cotswolds Diamond Way, a long-distance footpath linking Ebrington to Adlestrop and taking in some of the picturesque villages of the region including Chipping Campden, Northleach and Bourton-on-the-Water.

COLN ROGERS

To the south-west of Northleach, the village takes its name from the river on which it stands and from the knight Roger de Gloster who gave it to the monks of Gloucester abbey before his death in 1106.

≈

In 1541, after the Dissolution of the Monasteries, the village passed into the hands of the Dean and Chapter of Gloucester cathedral. The parish church of St Andrew is a hidden gem that preserves many of its original features including parts of the nave and chancel. The frame for one of the windows in the north side is made out of a single piece of stone. The simple stone pulpit dates from

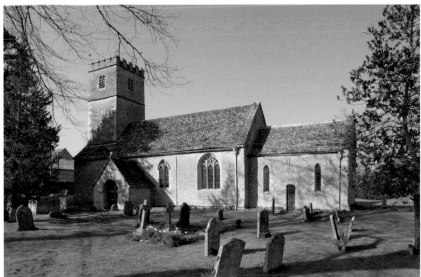

the 15th century. A beautiful plaque inside the porch of the church commemorates the fact that Coln Rogers is a "thankful village", where all the men from the village who served in the First World War returned alive. The village is situated at an idyllic point where the river Coln starts to broaden on its way south from the high wolds to the flatter lands below. On either side of the valley are some fine woodlands which can be enjoyed on a stroll along the peaceful banks of the river.

CRANHAM

At the head of a valley, Cranham, just south-east of Gloucester, enjoys excellent views with access to a large common to the south and extensive beech woods to the north.

The parish church of St James the Great is in the south-eastern part of the village and dominates the surrounding countryside. It was built largely in the 15th century when the area prospered as a result of sheep-rearing. This is commemorated on the church itself by two pairs of sheep shears carved onto the second stage of the church tower. Inside the church there is an early 16th century rood screen, a tripartite reredos and a monument to Obadiah Done who was rector to the parish for 57 years. Beyond the beech woods is Prinknash Abbey which houses a small

community of Benedictine monks. The composer Gustav Holst lived briefly in Cranham and whilst there he wrote what is probably the best known tune for Christina Rossetti's Christmas carol *In the Bleak Midwinter*. The tune is called "Cranham" and the house where he stayed is now called "Midwinter Cottage". The Cotswold Way footpath from Chipping Campden to Bath passes close to the village.

DUNTISBOURNE ABBOTS

This small, neat village is situated in the valley of the river Dunt. Its name comes from the fact that it was once owned by the abbots of Gloucester.

Duntisbourne Abbots did not have a lord of the manor living in the village until the 19th century. It was acquired by the locally powerful Pleydell family in the mid 18th century and Duntisbourne House was later occupied by Dr Matthew Baillie, a

former physician to George III. The village church of St Peter dates from the 12th century but it is built on the site of an earlier Saxon structure. The Norman tower has a low saddleback roof and the 13th century belfry lights feature pierced stone lattice-work. The interior contains a late Norman font and an unusually con-structed chancel arch added during the restoration of 1872. Access to the churchyard is through a pictur-esque lych-gate. The Hoar Stone long barrow, a chambered tomb set on a long mound, can be found about a mile to the south.

DUNTISBOURNE LEER

Close to Duntisbourne Abbots is Duntisbourne Leer. Like its neighbour it takes its name from the abbey that once owned it. In this case the hamlet was the property of Lire abbey in Normandy.

The hamlet's French ownership came to an end in 1416 when it was given to the monks of Cirencester abbey. At the Dissolution of the Monasteries Duntisbourne Leer was acquired by the Pleydell family with whom it continued until the late 19th century.

Today the hamlet consists of two farmhouses and various outbuildings grouped around a clear and shallow ford over the river Dunt. In the 19th century a number of Dissenters took up residence in the two villages. One of them, Elizabeth Cross, later set up a mission school on the Pacific island of Tonga. The mission was responsible for the conversion to Christianity of the King and Queen of Tonga who remain Methodists to the present day.

DUNTISBOURNE ROUSE

The third of the Duntisbourne villages takes its name from the Rouse family who were powerful in the area until the Wars of the Roses.

Standing in a sloping churchyard overlooking the Dunt valley, is the tiny church of St Michael and All Angels, which is striking for its simple and almost perfect proportions. The church has a Saxon nave and, because of the sloping ground, a small crypt chapel beneath the Norman chancel; this is an unusual element for such a small church. The crypt can be reached via external steps. The churchyard contains a 14th century cross with a mutilated head. Saxon herringbone stonework can be seen in the nave and there are some fine Norman windows. The solid 13th century font is complemented by late

medieval choir stalls and a medieval painting on the north chancel wall and crypt. Like Duntisbourne Abbots the tower has a saddleback roof. This quiet village is on the Macmillan Way which runs from here to the Dorset coast at Abbotsbury. There are many pleasant woodland walks in the area.

EASTLEACH

There are two villages at Eastleach 11 miles east of Cirencester,
Turville and Martin, which face each other across the river Leach.
The two villages once belonged to different manors.

The two Norman churches are 200 yards apart and the villages are connected by two bridges. One bridge carries the road but the other is an unusual construction of large flat stones. This footbridge is known as "Keble's bridge" and commemorates the Keble family who were lords of the manor of Eastleach Turville in the 16th century. The most famous Keble was John, the founder of the Oxford Movement, after whom Keble College Oxford is named. The peaceful aspect of today's villages makes it difficult to imagine that there were once anti-machinery riots here.

Above: the simple clapper bridge across the river, named after John Keble, rector of St Martin's and leader of the Oxford Movement. *Below*: the inviting beer garden of the Victoria Inn, formerly a private house with attached coach house.

EBRINGTON

The many springs in and around Ebrington, three miles east of Chipping Campden, meant it has been a favoured place of settlement since the Iron Age.

This pleasant village overlooks a valley watered by the Knee Brook as it makes its way to the river Stour. It would appear that people who settle in Ebrington don't like to leave; Ebrington Manor has been occupied continuously by the Fortescue family since 1456. The manor house has undergone successive renovations since the 15th century and its exterior is largely the result of 17th century alterations. Sharing a slight ridge above the village with the manor house is the church of St Eadburga. It preserves some Norman features, such as a geometric design on the tympanum, and some medieval ones such as a roundel window depicting the month of October. One of the monuments in the church is dedicated to William Kyte Esq and records his gift, in 1632, of "the milk of ten good and sufficient milch kine" to be distributed to the poor of Ebrington "from May 10th to November 1st in perpetuity". A note below the monument explains that the distribution of the Cow Charity was shifted from milk to cash in 1952.

FAIRFORD

*The jewel in Fairford's crown is the church of St Mary.
Constructed in the late Perpendicular style it celebrates
the wealth and power of the Tame family who built it out
of profits from the wool industry.*

During the Reformation Puritan reformers removed, or more
often smashed, much of the stained-glass that adorned parish
churches throughout the country. Fairford's stained-glass
windows somehow survived the Puritan purges and are a particularly fine example of late medieval work, coming from the
studios of Barnard Flower, glass painter to Henry VII. Within
the church an impressively sturdy oak-beamed roof is supported
on carved stone corbels and a series of misericords depicts scenes
of 15th century life. Other notable buildings in Fairford include
an early 18th century free school decorated with plaques to

esteemed teachers, the 17th century Bull Hotel, Fairford Mill and the Oxpen. Beyond the mill the town is on the eastern edge of the Cotswold Water Park, an extensive complex of over 140 lakes created from gravel extraction which now provide habitats for wildfowl. Fairford has been a market town since 1135 when Henry I granted permission for a twice weekly market to be held in the town.

FARMINGTON

The village of Farmington stands on high ground east of Northleach between the valleys of the river Leach and the Sherborne brook.

The principal house in the village is Farmington Lodge. This is a mixture of 18th and 19th century styles and is fronted by four sizeable Doric columns. A rather more graceful aspect of the village green is an octagonal pumphouse topped by an elegant cupola. The church is Norman in origin and still retains many Norman features such as its south doorway and chancel arch. The Perpendicular tower was added in the 15th century but fits in well with the earlier buildings. To the west of Farmington is Norbury Camp where there are both Iron and Stone Age remains.

GREAT BARRINGTON

Great Barrington, near Burford, began its life as an estate village and much of it remains so today. A great deal of the stone that makes the Cotswolds so distinctive was quarried in the area surrounding this village.

Barrington Park was originally the seat of the Bray family but it became the property of Earl Talbot, Lord Chancellor in the reign of George II. The house was rebuilt in the Palladian style in 1738 and most of the park was landscaped at this time. Little of the house can be seen from the road but there is a fine set of ornamental gates on the road which enters the village from the north.

The estate fell into decline in the 1960s and 1970s but this has now largely been reversed. The church at Great Barrington is mostly Norman and contains some interesting monuments including one depicting two children of the Bray family being led towards heaven by an angel.

GUITING POWER

Guiting Power lies near the confluence of the river Windrush and one of its tributaries. Its name comes from a mixture of the old English term "gyte", meaning an outpouring of water, and the name of the Le Poer family, the village's 13th century owners.

The majority of houses in Guiting Power are clustered around a sloping village green with the village's war memorial at its centre. The local stone and centuries of vernacular architecture give the varied buildings an exceptional sense of unity. To the south of the village is the parish church of St Michael; this still possesses imposing

Norman north and south doorways but the interior suffers from a rather austere Victorian restoration. Guiting Power hosts a small but significant music festival every July and it is a popular starting point for walks along the Windrush valley, into Guiting Woods or towards Naunton or Hawling.

Above: sheep gathered close to a drystone wall south of the village. The pastoral scenery of the Cotswolds – close-cropped pastures enclosed by drystone walls – has resulted from centuries of sheep-farming.
Left: Castlett Farm, north of the village.

HAMPNETT

The village of Hampnett, 11 miles south-east of Cheltenham, is scattered around a large village green. The village lies close to the source of the river Leach.

St George's church is largely Norman in its architecture but during the 1880s its interior was decorated with extensive stencil work. Purists might complain that these designs obscure the clean lines of the Norman church but on the other hand, during the Norman and medieval periods, most churches would have had similarly decorated walls. In some ways St George's might be more Norman than most churches; for the observant

there are some fine carvings of birds on the capitals supporting the chancel that date back to the original building. Hampnett is on the Macmillan Way and has many fine walks leading from it, either following the valley of the Leach or over the nearby hills towards Yanworth.

Hazleton

Close to Hampnett, Hazleton's position gives it excellent views over the surrounding countryside.

The relative isolation of its setting means that Hazleton has changed little in recent years but the ancient Salt Way used to pass through it and it prospered during the medieval period as a result of the wool trade. The parish church is a Norman foundation but its tower and windows belong to the later Perpendicular period. Internally the south doorway and chancel arch are Norman and there is a very solid 13th century baptismal font. As in ancient times there is a great deal of foot and horse traffic around the village as it

offers excellent bridleways to Salperton in the north, Notgrove to the north-east and Turkdean to the east. "Turkdean Barrow near Hazleton" has the distinction of being learnedly discussed by Indiana Jones in *Raiders of the Lost Ark*.

HIDCOTE

Made up of two separate hamlets, Hidcote Bartrim and Hidcote Boyce are four miles north-east of Chipping Campden. The village is famous for the National Trust owned gardens of Hidcote Manor.

The 17th century Hidcote Manor was acquired in 1907 by the family of Major Lawrence Johnston. At that time its gardens consisted of little more than a few fields but once Johnston became interested they quickly grew in both size and scope so that by the 1920s Johnston employed 12 full-time gardeners. Rather than laying out a single garden Johnston created a series of them separated by walls and trees. He was also prepared to scour the world for exotic plants and either led or sponsored plant-collecting expeditions to the Swiss Alps, the Andes, Burma, Kenya and many other places. After devoting more than 40 years to his passion Major Johnston donated the gardens to the National Trust in 1948. The highlights of today's gardens include the White Garden, the Bathing Pool Garden and the Fuchsia Garden but the site also contains wild gardens, a kitchen garden, grass walks and a theatre lawn where an open-air production of Shakespeare takes place each summer.

LITTLE BARRINGTON

The sloping, hollowed out village green in Little Barrington, three miles west of Burford, is on the site of one of the quarries that supplied the Cotswolds with its distinctive stone.

Veneration for the famous Cotswold stone can be seen in the construction of some of the cottages which incorporate original medieval doorways into their structures. The village also produced one of the most famous stonemasons of the 17th century: Thomas Strong, who worked with Sir

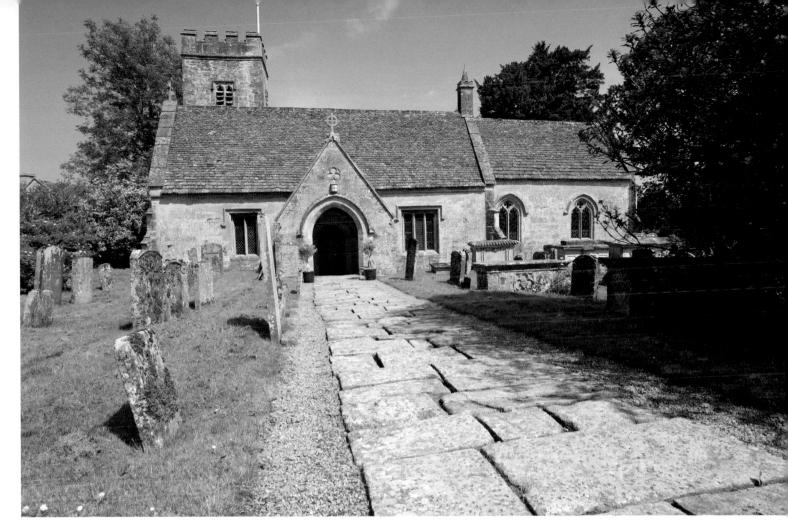

Christopher Wren on St Paul's cathedral and many other London churches. Little Barrington's own church is Norman in origin and has a number of distinctive features. The bridge to the east of the village owes its existence to a bequest by Thomas Strong for a bridge that would be wide enough to allow two men to carry a corpse across it in safety.

LOWER SLAUGHTER

*The neighbouring villages of Upper and Lower Slaughter are just north
of Bourton-on-theWater. Both villages are sited on the river Eye, which is known locally
as Slaughter Brook.*

Several footbridges span the river Eye here and there is a 19th century corn mill with a working waterwheel at one end of the village. The mill is now a museum. Lower Slaughter village hall was built in 1887 and provides an interesting late Victorian attempt at a traditional Cotswold style. Also dating from the 19th century is St Mary's church which was rebuilt in 1867. It has an imposing spire but there is little else of interest in the building apart from some 13th century arches from the original church between the nave and south aisle. Lower Slaughter Manor House dates back to 1650 when it was built for Valentine Strong, the owner of the quarry at Little Barrington. The house has been remodelled since its construction but its grounds preserve one of the largest dovecotes in Gloucestershire. To the east of the house is a fine stable block.

MARSHFIELD

Marshfield benefits from its proximity to Bath and Bristol and has been a market town since 1234.

In the Middle Ages Marshfield was one of the largest towns in the area and its prosperity continued well into the 18th century. By then it was particularly concerned with the malt trade as can be seen in the many malthouses and long storage buildings at the back of some properties. There are many listed buildings in the town but the almshouses established by the Crispe family between 1612 and 1619 are particularly interesting. The eight gabled houses are arranged on either side of a chapel which has a small spire and front porch. Originally each house consisted of a single room with a stone spiral staircase in one corner leading to a bedroom.

MINCHINHAMPTON

This attractive village, two miles south-east of Stroud, was once one of the most important cloth towns in the Cotswolds.

Minchinhampton is located on high land between the Golden valley and the Nailsworth valley. The square is dominated by a 17th century Market House which is supported on sturdy stone pillars. Nearby is a post office housed in a genuine Queen Anne building. The church has an interesting truncated spire and parts of it date from the 12th century. Of particular interest is the 14th century south transept which contains a varied collection of tomb recesses and effigies in the Decorated style. The 600 acre Minchinhampton Common was granted to the people of the village in the 16th century. The common is now owned and managed by the National Trust and its high location makes it a popular destination for ramblers.

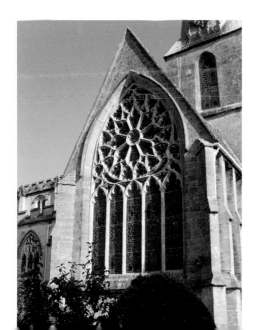

MINSTER LOVELL

Minster Lovell, three miles west of Witney, combines an idyllic rural setting with buildings that reflect the village's varied past.

A bridge across the Windrush leads to a high street that has a well balanced selection of thatched cottages and other Cotswold stone houses. St Kenelm's church was built in 1431 and has an attractive vaulted ceiling underneath the central tower. It is believed that some of the stained-glass is original and there is a fine alabaster knight's tomb, probably that of William, the 7th Baron of Lovell, who built the church and nearby manor house. Minster Lovell Hall was once a fortified manor house but it was dismantled to provide stone for nearby farm buildings. Also worth noting is the round medieval dovecote.

MISERDEN

Six miles north-east of Stroud, this ancient parish has buildings from many periods, including a ruined castle and dower house.

Near to the village are the earthworks of a motte and bailey castle which would have been erected shortly after the Norman Conquest. The name Miserden is a corruption of the name of the family, la Musarder, who held the manor from the 12th century onwards. Among the surviving 17th century houses are the rectory, Lampacre Cottage and a pair of cottages, one of which used to be the blacksmith's. The two-storey dower house dates from the 18th century and had an east wing added in the 1860s by Sir John Rolt. Sir John also rebuilt other parts of the village. The church has late Saxon origins although it was extensively restored in the 1880s. The war memorial was designed by Sir Edwin Lutyens who also carried out work at Miserden Park, a large Elizabethan mansion with exquisite gardens just to the east of the village. A comparatively recent feature is a small octagonal shelter built around a large sycamore tree in the village centre.

Moreton-in-Marsh

Situated on the watershed between the rivers Thames and Severn, Moreton-in-Marsh has been a market centre for over 1000 years.

Moreton-in-Marsh started out as a Saxon settlement around the church, but it was redeveloped as a market in the 1220s. Charles I granted the town a market charter in 1637, which is still exercised every Tuesday. The development of turnpike roads in the 18th century increased the town's prosperity and many buildings in the High Street date from this period. In 1941 a bomber pilot training school opened nearby and this is now the country's largest training centre for fire-fighters. At the corner of Old Street there is a 16th century curfew tower. The bell was rung each night until the 1860s to tell people to return to their homes.

Above: the busy market takes place in the wide High Street, part of the Fosse Way, every Tuesday and attracts at least 200 stalls. *Above and left*: views of the Redesdale Market Hall, which stands on an island in the centre of the High Street. *Right*: the beautiful church of St David in the town centre was rebuilt in 1858.

NAUNTON

The village of Naunton lies in the upper Windrush valley and can often be seen in its entirety from nearby hills.

The village has been a centre for sheep-rearing since it became monastic land in the Middle Ages. This long history of animal husbandry means that this part of the Windrush valley is home to flowers which grow only on unimproved limestone pasture. In particular cowslips can be found in the spring, whilst yellow rattle and orchids adorn the fields in summer. Naunton's other industry was the production of stone roofing slates; at one time 30,000 a week were dug from thin stone seams in nearby mines. The church has an imposing Perpendicular tower complete with pinnacles and gargoyles. In the interior there is a carved 15th century stone pulpit and a font dating from about the same period. Naunton's dovecote, erected in 1660, incorporates four gables around a central turret.

NORTHLEACH

Northleach was one of the most important Cotswold wool towns in the Middle Ages. Its heyday as a medieval trading centre can still be glimpsed in its market square and many beautiful half-timbered buildings.

The most obvious legacy of Northleach's pre-eminence in the wool trade is the church of St Peter and Paul. Largely rebuilt in the Perpendicular style in the 15th century, it is a magnificent example of the style and period. The south porch is said to be without equal in England and the pinnacled tower combines both elegance and strength. The generous windows in the clerestory provide ample light for such features as a 15th century goblet-shaped pulpit and a new ceiling designed by Sir Basil Spence. The church also has an extensive collection of brasses which commemorate the wool merchants whose wealth made the church possible. Elsewhere in the town there are other examples of civic pride and benefaction such as two sets of almshouses, one of which was exclusively for women, and a late 18th century "house of correction". The prison was built by local philanthropist Sir William Blackburn under the direction of the reformer Sir Onesiphorus Paul.

Left: the magnificent church of St Peter and St Paul is often referred to as "the cathedral of the Cotswolds". *Above*: many beautiful brass rubbings of local wool merchants grace its interior, and the graveyard is filled with their tombstones.

PAINSWICK

The stream in the valley below Painswick once provided power for its woollen mills whilst the purity of its water made the village an important centre for cloth dyeing.

✦

Many of the houses in the village date from the 17th and 18th centuries and once belonged to wealthy wool merchants. The clear, fast-flowing streams that tumble down the steep slopes that surround the village were ideal for powering the fulling mills central to the production of cloth. At the heart of the

village is a fine church which combines sections from the 15th century with an elegant 17th century tower. Surrounding the church are well-tended colonnades of yew trees which have been in place since 1792. Legend has it that there are only 99 trees as the devil always kills the hundredth. In September each year the Painswick "clypping" ceremony is held. This has nothing to do with keeping the yews in check but takes its name from the Old English word *clyppan* meaning to embrace. Groups of children form a circle around the church then approach and retreat three times while singing a hymn. A cake containing a porcelain dog called "puppy dog pie" is baked at this time.

THE RISSINGTONS

Great Rissington, Little Rissington and Wyck Rissington are three small
villages near Bourton-on-the-Water. Each has its own church.

Perhaps the most famous of the three villages is Little Rissington. The RAF flying
school was just outside the village in the Second World War and memorials in
St Peter's churchyard commemorate the many pilots who died. After the war RAF
Little Rissington served as the headquarters of the Red Arrows aerial display team.
The village has a number of fine houses and some picturesque wells. Wyck
Rissington's claim to fame is the fact that the composer Gustav Holst was given
his first professional position as an organist at the church of St Lawrence. One
of the vicars at the church, Canon Henry Cheaves, built a maze between the rectory
and the church to symbolise the Christian path through life. The maze has been
removed but the Canon's memorial in the church records its shape. Also worth

seeking out here is the grave of a traveller, James Loveridge, whose life ended in the village. Great Rissington is a modest village, despite its name, but it does possess a fine 17th century manor house and the sensitively restored church of St John the Baptist. It dates from the 1200s but the tower, with its pinnacles and battlements, was built in the 15th century.

SAINTBURY

This small village, three miles west of Chipping Campden, is ranged along the side of Saintbury Hill and has fine views over the Vale of Evesham.

It is thought that the name Saintbury refers to a holy man called Cada who built a small cell near the position of the present church during the Saxon period. The church of St Nicholas dates from Norman times but some fragments of a former Saxon building are still preserved; for example, the primitive Anglo-Saxon sundial mounted over a doorway in the south wall. The interior features a Jacobean altar rail and pulpit and a Queen Anne period barrel-vaulted roof. The spire has a six bell peal. The church even seems to preserve a pre-Christian relic in the form of a *Sheila-na-gig*, a Celtic fertility goddess, which is built into the sanctuary wall. The village itself features a fine cross which stands at the crossroads to the north of the village. The lower part dates from the 15th century whilst the Maltese cross and sundial were added in 1848.

SHEEPSCOMBE

Sheepscombe is situated in a narrow valley tucked into the Cotswold escarpment two miles east of Painswick.

The word "combe" in the name of the village means valley. It was originally the site of a deer park and hunting ground but in the 17th century it benefited from the growth of the textile industry. Many of the houses in the village date from this period. Woollen mills were also introduced but decline followed in the late 18th and early 19th centuries; the last mill closed in 1839. The village church of St John the Apostle was built and opened in 1820 and has stained-glass windows by William Morris. The village school opened in 1822 and was modernised in 1882. To the east of Sheepscombe is beautiful Workman's Wood, a site of special scientific interest.

SHERBORNE

Three miles east of Northleach, the village developed in the Middle Ages because its plentiful water supply made it an ideal centre for sheep-shearing.

In the Middle Ages there was little else in Sherborne apart from sheep and the Abbot of Winchcombe's summer palace. With the Dissolution of the Monasteries the land passed to the Dutton family and by 1651 Sherborne House had been built. The present Sherborne grew up as an estate village for Sherborne House. The Dutton family remained in residence until the 1980s when the estate was bequeathed to the National Trust. Sherborne House, which was extensively rebuilt in the 19th century, is now divided into luxury flats and the rest of the estate is dedicated to improved access to the land and nature conservation. Sherborne church, near the park, is chiefly interesting for its many monuments and memorials to the Dutton family.

SLAD

Slad is a small village that straggles along the side of a valley near Stroud. It was the childhood home of the author Laurie Lee.

Life in the village in the 1920s is brilliantly evoked in Laurie Lee's 1959 autobiography *Cider with Rosie* but the present village has not let literary fame go to its head. It remains remarkably unspoiled and it is still possible to gain a sense of the village described by Laurie Lee; for instance, The Woolpack inn, mentioned in the book, is still trading. The earliest references to Slad come from 1353 when a bridge was built there to cross Slad brook. The oldest building is probably Steanbridge House, an early 17th century gabled clothier's house. Some weavers' cottages also date from this period but the church of the Holy Trinity and the village school were built in the 1830s. In the 19th century the three main mills in the valley – Steanbridge, Hazel Mill and New Mills – ceased production. Laurie Lee, who immortalised this corner of the Cotswolds, is buried in the graveyard of the village church.

SNOWSHILL

There have been settlements near Snowshill, three miles south of Broadway, since the Bronze Age. A round barrow near the village contained a famous collection of weapons and other artefacts now in the British Museum.

Snowshill was owned by Winchcombe abbey from 821 until the Dissolution of the Monasteries when it was given to King Henry VIII's sixth wife, Katherine Parr. The main part of the current Snowshill Manor House dates from around 1500 but there were alterations and extensions in the 17th and 18th centuries. In 1919 the almost derelict building was bought and restored by Charles Paget Wade, who needed somewhere to display his collection of 22,000 examples of craftsmanship. Amassed between 1900 and 1951 the collection is extremely diverse and is intended to illustrate Wade's idea that each object embodies the spirit of the craftsman who made

it and the age in which it was produced. Wade assembled articles from many different times and countries and included such things as automatons, butter stamps, bicycles, children's toys, clocks, cow bells, locks and even 26 suits of Samurai armour. Wade designed the garden around the house in collaboration with the Arts & Crafts architect M H Baillie-Scott who laid out its terraces and ponds between 1920 and 1923. The Manor was donated to the National Trust in 1951.

SOUTHROP

Southrop is a pleasant village on the river Leach which was once owned by Wadham College Oxford.

⤝

The village's most famous inhabitant was John Keble, the founder of the Oxford Movement for the reform of the Church of England. Keble was working as a curate in Southrop when he formulated the movement's basic principles with three friends. The church of St Peter is a plain and simple building with a long and varied history. The main part dates from around 1100 and

is mostly Norman in style, whilst the 13th century chancel is in early English style. Some remodelling took place in 1852. The most impressive feature of the church is the carved Norman font which is said to be one of the finest in the country; each of its panels represents a virtue triumphing over a vice.

STANTON

Stanton is claimed to be one of the oldest settlements in the Cotswolds.

❧

South-west of Broadway, most of the houses in Stanton date from the 17th century but the village was extensively restored by the architect Sir Philip Stott after he purchased large tracts of it just

before the First World War. Stott modernised many features and even introduced buildings from elsewhere, including three timber-framed barns, but set up covenants to prevent the worst excesses of the 20th century from taking hold in the village. His work means that Stanton often provides a backdrop for period films and television programmes. Parts of Stanton's church date back to the 12th century and it features both a 14th century and a Jacobean pulpit. It has an elegant spire and some of its windows date from the 15th century.

STANWAY

One mile south of Stanton, the small village of Stanway is dominated by the gatehouse to Stanway House where a mixture of architectural styles are given unity by the local stone.

Almost all of the stone used in Stanway comes from nearby Coscombe Quarry. Stanway House was built during the 1580s on the site of an earlier manor house. It is mostly Jacobean in style and has a remarkable 60-pane full-height bay window. The grounds contain a restored water garden which features the highest fountain in England, an impressive

tithe barn dating from 1370 and a log-fired brewing house. The church of St Peter retains its Jacobean pulpit but elsewhere has suffered badly at the hands of Victorian restorers. Opposite the drive to Stanway House is a thatched cricket pavilion mounted on saddle stones. This unusual building was a gift to the village by J M Barrie, author of *Peter Pan*, a frequent visitor to the area in the early years of the 20th century.

STOW-ON-THE-WOLD

Stow-on-the-Wold is the highest town in the Cotswolds; the shape of its unusual market square is in part dictated by the need for stallholders to be protected from the wind.

"Stow-on-the-Wold, where the wind blows cold" – so goes the old rhyme, referring to the town's position on the top of a hill between the valleys of the Evenlode and

the Dikler. Stow-on-the-Wold has been a thriving market town since at least 1107 when it received its first Royal Grant. By the 15th century there were two annual fairs and Daniel Defoe reported the sale of 20,000 sheep there in the 18th century. Evidence of the town's prosperity can be seen in the parish church of St Edward which was built between the 11th and the 15th centuries and restored in the 1680s and again in 1847. Its tower, completed in 1447, is 88ft high and houses the heaviest peal of bells in Gloucestershire. The current church clock was made in 1926 but there have been clocks on the tower since 1580. The town stocks go back to the 15th century and, like the church clocks, they have been replaced on several occasions. Stow-on-the Wold was the site of one of the last major battles of the Civil War. A royalist march on Oxford with 3,000 men was thwarted by Cromwell and 1,000 men were imprisoned in the church.

TAYNTON

This compact Oxfordshire village stands on the border between Gloucestershire and Oxfordshire. Confusingly there is also a Taynton in Gloucestershire.

Taynton stone, quarried nearby, was highly prized during the Middle Ages and early modern period and can be found in local buildings, Oxford colleges and many of Sir Christopher Wren's London churches. Taynton church dates from 1450 and is unusual in being in the Decorated style rather than Perpendicular. Given the importance of stone to Taynton's parishioners it is not surprising to find some excellent stone carving in the church. The font consists of an octagonal bowl with kneeling angels at each corner and figures of beasts, Evangelists and a mermaid in between. There are also vividly carved corbel heads in the nave and north transept which show off the elaborate headwear of the late medieval period. Two carved figures in the north transept are thought to be King Henry VI and the Abbot of Tewkesbury.

TEMPLE GUITING

Temple Guiting is situated on the river Windrush not far from Guiting Power. The Temple portion of its name dates back to the 12th century when the manor was owned by the Knights Templar.

St Mary's church in Temple Guiting is built in an unusual, but not displeasing, combination of medieval and Georgian classical styles. An outstanding feature of the medieval church are the elaborate carvings on the corbel table and around the outside of the chancel; these represent real and imaginary animals, religious figures, and human likenesses. In the Georgian section there is an ornately painted decalogue over the south door. This set of wooden panels, representing the Ten Commandments, the Creed and the Lord's Prayer dates from 1748 but has only recently been restored. Temple Guiting Manor House was described by Pevsner as "one of the finest, if not the very best of the small Cotswold Tudor manor houses."

TETBURY

Its strategic position close to the Fosse Way between Cirencester and Bath helped Tetbury become an important market town.

In the centre of Tetbury is the Market House, built in 1655. Close by is The Chipping, where a livestock market was held amongst an imposing collection of

18th and 19th century buildings. The well-worn Chipping Steps lead down to the ancient remains of a Cistercian priory. Also in this area is Gumstool Hill where the annual Woolsack Races take place every Spring Bank Holiday Monday. St Mary's church is an imposing

building rebuilt in the Gothic style in the late 18th century; its spire is 186ft high. The interior is illuminated by graceful Perpendicular windows and features box pews, panelled galleries and two magnificent chandeliers. Tetbury's original Court House now houses a Police Museum which tells the story of the Gloucestershire police constabulary since its founding in 1839.

Upper Slaughter

Although it sounds bloodthirsty the name "Slaughter" is probably derived from the Old English word "slohtre" meaning slough or boggy place.

Upper Slaughter is situated one mile upstream from its sister village of Lower Slaughter, 15 miles east of Cheltenham on the tiny river Eye. The village stands on a hillside above the stream and is grouped around a small square with the church alongside. The cottages that comprise the square were remodelled by Sir Edwin Lutyens in 1906.

Crossing the river are a number of stone footbridges and a ford. A motte and bailey castle once overlooked the site but there is very little of this still to be seen. The most imposing building today is the gabled Manor House, parts of which date from the 15th century; the front is an Elizabethan addition. St Peter's church has Norman origins and a 15th century tower. Completely belying its name, Upper Slaughter is a double "thankful village" – all the men it sent to fight in the First and Second World Wars returned home alive.

WILLERSEY

*With its spacious village green, its duckpond and ancient church, Willersey is
a typical English village situated two miles north of Broadway.*

One of four villages lying along the foot of the
north-west escarpment between Broadway and
Meon Hill, Willersey is on the very edge of the
Cotswolds. Its mellow-stoned, well-proportioned
houses link it firmly with the uplands. There were
Iron Age settlements near the present village and
its existence is recorded in the Domesday Book.
In the Middle Ages the abbots of Evesham had a

summer residence in Willersey and, after the
Dissolution of the Monasteries, William Roper,
the son-in-law of Sir Thomas More, held the
manor. At the Restoration King Charles II gave
the Penderel family a house in Willersey in thanks
for their help in his escape after the Battle of
Worcester. Most of the houses in the village date
from this period or later. The village school was

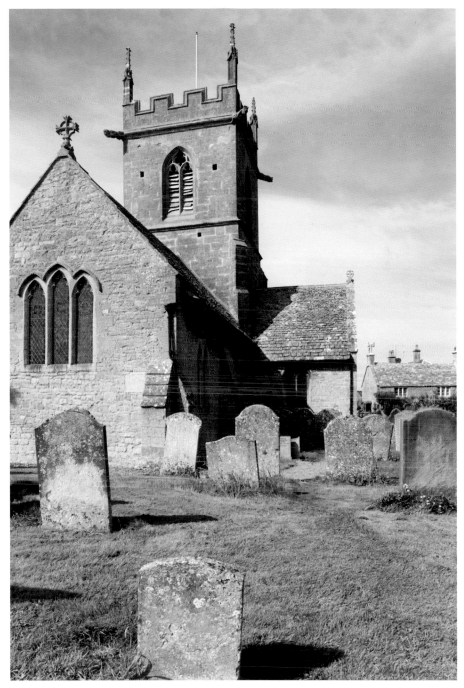

erected in 1844. St Peter's church dates largely from the 14th century and has a prominent central tower, battlements, pinnacles and outstanding gargoyles. The church was re-roofed and restored during the Victorian period. The annual Willersey Wake, held around June 24 on the village green, is a central feature of Willersey life. The village benefits from two excellent pubs – the magnificent 17th century Bell Inn, overlooking the duckpond and the New Inn on Main Street which serves locally-produced beers.

WINCHCOMBE

Situated on a slope at the foot of Langley Hill, eight miles north-east of Cheltenham, Winchcombe's pretty streets lead down to the river Isbourne.

The town that can be seen today is largely the legacy of the Cotswolds wool trade and St Peter's, at its centre, is a fine example of a "wool" church. The original church was rebuilt between 1460 and 1470 and major restoration took place during the Victorian period. The west tower has three stages and is surmounted by battlements, pinnacles and gargoyles. A series of grotesque heads adorn many parts of the exterior and a gilded weathercock was added in 1874. Inside the

church a rather sad wall-mounted memorial to Thomas Williams of Corndean, who died in 1636, shows a kneeling effigy in painted stone. The figure of his wife, who re-married after his death, was never added. On the edge of the village is Sudeley Castle, the former home of Katherine Parr, the last wife of Henry VIII, and the Civil War headquarters of Prince Rupert. The almost derelict castle was acquired by the Dent family in 1837 and Emma Dent did much to conserve both the castle and other historical monuments in the area. In 1887 Emma Dent provided Winchcombe with its first piped water supply to celebrate Queen Victoria's Golden Jubilee.

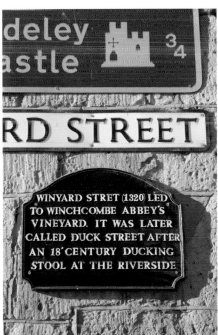

WOTTON-UNDER-EDGE

*Wotton-under-Edge, 11 miles south-west of Stroud, is a town whose buildings are scattered over a
wide area rather than being clustered around a central square or green.*

This ancient town stands on a ridge of high ground above the
Severn valley, surrounded by a steep wooded escarpment. It was
destroyed by fire in the reign of King John and rebuilt in 1253.
The oldest building is the timber-framed Ram Inn which is
believed to date from 1350. The parish church of St Mary the
Virgin was consecrated in 1283 and possesses a fine late 14th
century tower. Inside the church is the Berkeley Tomb, an early
15th century table tomb which bears life-size brasses of Thomas,
10th Baron de Berkeley (1352-1417) and his wife, Margaret. The
brasses are reputedly the best of their kind in England. The
church has an 18th century organ which originally came from
St Martin-in-the-Fields, in London. Built for George I it was

reputedly first played by Handel. Wotton Grammar School was founded by Katharine Lady Berkeley in 1384. The comprehensive school in the town is named after her. The Church Street Almshouses were built in 1638. One notable resident of Wotton was Sir Isaac Pitman who lived in a house that still stands in Orchard Street. Here he invented his system of shorthand in 1837.

WINDRUSH

Five miles west of Burford, the village is named after the river Windrush, the tributary of the Thames on which it stands.

Windrush is a former quarrying village and possesses many fine houses built from the local stone. A few of the houses date from the 17th century and one is dated 1668. St Peter's church is of Norman origin and has been the parish church since 1586. The south doorway is elaborately carved with slightly menacing looking beaked heads which are mixed with the heads of other fantastical beasts. In the churchyard there is a finely decorated "Wool Bale" tomb, which represents the source of the deceased's wealth in the form of corded bales of wool. The interior of the church is far less interesting due to over enthusiastic 19th century restoration. South of the village is the Iron Age hillfort of Windrush Camp of which only the banks can be seen.